FAMOUS PEOPLE
FAMOUS LIVES

Biographies of famous people to support
the National Curriculum.

Anne Frank

by Harriet Castor

Illustrated by Helena Owen

W

First Published in 1996 by Franklin Watts
This edition 2001

Franklin Watts
338 Euston Road, London NW1 3BH

Franklin Watts Australia
Level 17/207 Kent Street
Sydney, NSW 2000

© 1996 text Harriet Castor
© 1996 illustrations Helen Owen

ISBN 978 0 7496 4312 6

A CIP catalogue record for this book is
available from the British Library

Dewey Decimal Classification
Number: 940.54

Series Editor: Sarah Ridley
Designer: Kirstie Billingham
Consultant: Dr. Anne Millard
            and David Wray

We thank the Anne Frank Foundation in
Basle, Switzerland, for the basic rights

Printed in China

Franklin Watts is a division of Hachette
Children's Books, an Hachette
UK company.
www.hachette.co.uk

Anne Frank

Anne Frank lived with her
parents, her older sister Margot,
and their cat in a flat in
Amsterdam, in the Netherlands.

Anne was bright and chatty,
with lots of friends.

Anne and her family were German – and they were Jewish, too. They had left Germany when it was taken over by a man called Adolf Hitler and his followers, the Nazis.

Hitler hated Jews and wanted
to kill them all.

In June 1942, Anne had her thirteenth birthday.

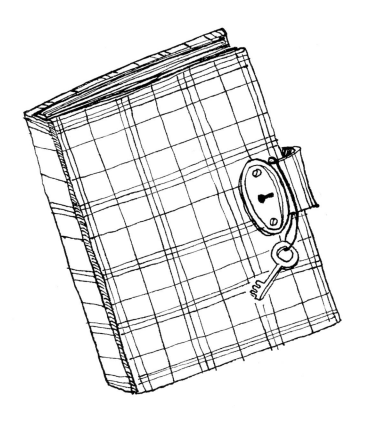

She got a jigsaw puzzle, a
brooch, some books and some
sweets. But the best present of
all was a diary. Anne had
never had one before. She
was delighted!

Anne started writing in her
diary. She made up a friend
called 'Kitty', and wrote letters
to her, describing her happy life
in Amsterdam.

Anne carried on writing to Kitty for the next two years, but during that time her life changed a great deal.

It was wartime. Hitler had sent his army to invade other countries in Europe. People fought against them but the

Germans carried on. When they invaded the Netherlands, life soon became very difficult for the Jewish people there.

Hitler made lots of laws against Jews.

They had to wear yellow stars. They couldn't have jobs. They weren't allowed bicycles or cars. They couldn't go out after eight o'clock at night, even just to sit in their own gardens.

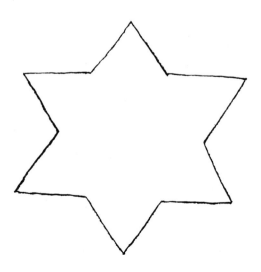

Then the Nazis started taking Jews away to terrible places, called concentration camps, and a letter came to the Franks' flat saying that they wanted to take Margot.

Anne's parents didn't want Margot to go. They were afraid of what would happen to her. They decided the whole family had to hide from the Nazis.

Where shall we hide?

Don't worry – everything's arranged.

Anne couldn't take a suitcase
in case the Nazis got suspicious.
So she packed a few belongings
in her satchel, and put on as
many clothes as she could.

She wore a dress, a skirt,
a jacket, some shorts, three
pairs of pants, two vests and
much more!

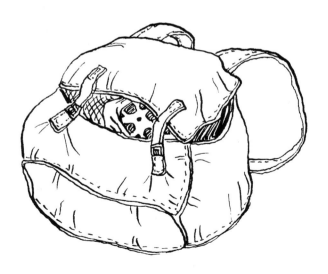

Then Anne's family went to live in the hiding place.

Mr Frank had prepared some rooms in the building where he used to work. They were at the back, upstairs. The entrance to them was hidden behind a bookcase.

In her diary, Anne called the place the Secret Annex.

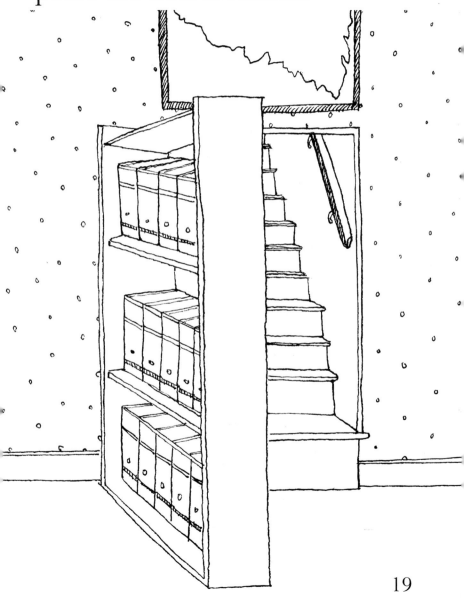

Keeping the Annex a secret was very important, so Mr Frank told only a few of the office workers about it. They promised to help.

One of them was Miep Gies. Miep brought the Franks food, books and news from the outside world.

Life in the Annex was strange.
Anne described it in her diary.

During the day, when there were
office workers downstairs, the
Franks had to be very quiet.
They couldn't flush a toilet or
run a tap until the workers went
home for the night.

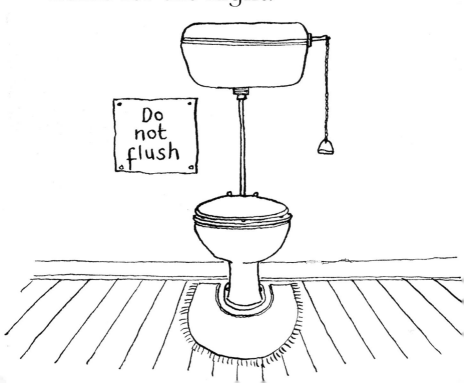

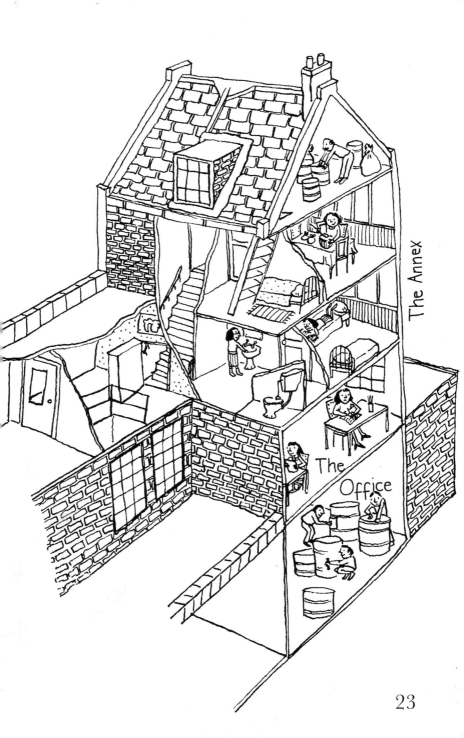

The Annex

The Office

23

Anne found it hard having to be
quiet all the time. She longed to
go outside, and laugh and play
in the sunshine.

24

Anne often quarrelled with her mother and Margot. Sometimes she felt her diary was her only good friend.

Soon, another Jewish family came to hide with the Franks: Mr and Mrs Van Daan and their son Peter. Later an eighth person joined them: a dentist called Mr Dussel.

Anne had to share a room with
Mr Dussel, which she didn't
like at all.

Anne, Margot and Peter Van Daan carried on with their lessons while they were in hiding. They hoped they'd soon be back at school, and they didn't want to get behind.

Anne loved history, but she hated maths!

Peter was two-and-a-half years older than Anne. At first she thought he was boring.

As the months went by she
changed her mind. Peter
became Anne's special friend.
For a while Anne even felt she
was in love with him.

All this time, Anne carried on writing her diary.

She decided she wanted to be a writer when she grew up. As well as her diary, she began writing stories. She hoped one day they would be published.

The Franks, the Van Daans and Mr Dussel lived in the Secret Annex for more than two years.

Anne grew a lot, but it was very hard to get new clothes. She wrote in her diary that her vests were so small they didn't even cover her tummy!

35

Several times while Anne and
her family were in hiding, the
offices downstairs were burgled.
Each time, everyone in the
Secret Annex was terrified that
the burglars might find their

CRASH!

BANG

hiding place and tell the Nazis.

But nothing happened.

CRASH!

One day, though, the Nazis did
find out about the Secret Annex.
No one knows for sure who
told them.

Anne and her family heard shouting downstairs. It was the police. They had come to take everyone in the Annex away.

Later, Miep went to the Annex.
She found Anne's diary and
stories scattered on the floor.
She gathered them together
and took them home.

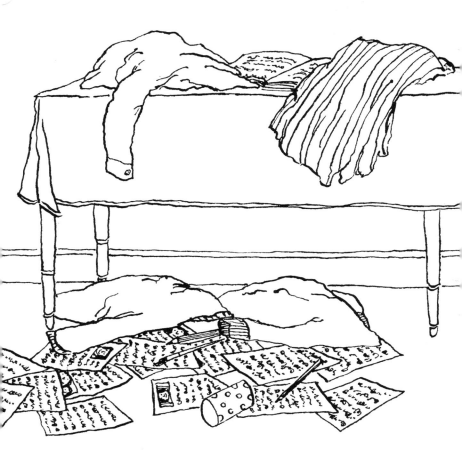

She didn't read them. Instead
she put them away in her desk,
ready to give back to Anne
when Anne came home after
the war.

But Anne never did come home.
She and her family were sent to
Nazi concentration camps.
There Anne died through lack
of food, warmth and shelter.

In less than a year, Margot,
Mrs Frank, Mr and Mrs Van
Daan, Peter and Mr Dussel
had all died too.

The only person from the Annex
to survive was Mr Frank. After
the war, he found his way to
Miep's home.

Miep gave Mr Frank Anne's diary and stories. He had never read them before.

Mr Frank let his friends read parts of Anne's diary too. They told him it was so good, he should have it published!

So in 1947, the first edition of Anne's diary went on sale. Her ambition to become a writer had come true, after all!

After the Story

Anne Frank is now more famous than she could ever have dreamt!

Her diary has been translated into 55 languages, and more than 25 million copies have been sold.

The Secret Annex has become a museum, and today you can still go and see the rooms where Anne and her family hid, and where Anne wrote her diary.

Lots of other Jews tried to hide from the Nazis. Some even lived under the floor boards of their houses!

Many, though, like Anne and her family, were betrayed and taken away.

Six million Jews were killed by the Nazis between 1938 and 1945. This is known as 'the Holocaust'.

Otto Frank lived until he was 91. He spent the rest of his life telling people about Anne's ideas. In spite of the war, Anne wrote about her belief in people's goodness and her hopes for peace.

Important Dates in Anne Frank's Lifetime

June 1929   Anne Frank is born in Frankfurt, Germany.

March 1933   Hitler becomes leader of Germany.

1933   Anne's family moves to Amsterdam, in the Netherlands.

1934   Anne goes to school.

1939 onwards   The Germans round up Jews and other groups and take them to concentration camps.

September 1939   Germany invades Poland. Britain and France declare war on Germany.

1940-41   Germany invades Denmark, Norway, Belgium, the Netherlands, France, Greece, Yugoslavia and the Soviet Union.

1941   America and Canada join the war against Japan and Germany.

June 1942   Otto Frank gives his daughter, Anne, a diary for her birthday.

July 1942   The Frank family moves into the Secret Annex to hide from the Germans.

1943 onwards   The war is changing. The Germans are not winning so many victories.

August 4, 1944   Police raid the Secret Annex and the Frank family are taken to concentration camps.

March 1945   Margot and Anne Frank die.

May 1945   Germany surrenders and war in Europe ends.

June 1945   Otto Frank returns to Amsterdam.

1947   The diary of Anne Frank is published.